All About Grandma
A Grandmother's Memory Keepsake Journal

This Journal Belongs To:

_____

Dedication

This Grandmother's Journal Log book is dedicated to all the precious Grandma's out there who have a story to share and want to tell their stories to their Grandchild.

You are my inspiration for producing books and I'm honored to be a part of keeping all of your notes and records organized.

This journal notebook will help you record your details about your life that need to be shared with your loved ones.

Thoughtfully put together with these sections to record:
Her Family Tree, Her Parents, Her Childhood, Her School-Age Years, Your Grandfather, Her Child/ Children, Family Traditions & Holidays, Family Recipes, Her Philosophy, Her Bucket List, Her Memories Of You, Her Letters To You & Photos.

How To Use this Book

The purpose of this book is to keep all of your Grandmother notes all in one place. It will help keep you organized.

This Grandmother's Journal will allow you to accurately document details about her life.

Here are examples of the prompts for you to fill in and write about your experience in this book:

1. Her Family Tree
2. Her Parents (Your Great-grandparents)
3. Her Childhood
4. Her School Age Years
5. Your Grandfather (Grandpa)
6. Her Child/Children (Your Mother or Father, Mom or Dad)
7. Family Traditions and Holidays
8. Family Recipes
9. Her Philosophy On Life and Words of Wisdom
10. Her Bucket List
11. Her Memories and Thoughts of You As a Baby/Child
12. Her Letters To You
13. Photos

Enjoy!

My Family Tree

Great-Grandmother	Great-Grandmother

Great-Grandfather	Great-Grandfather

My Grandmother	My Grandfather

My Mother

Me	My Sibling

My Family Tree

Great-Grandmother	Great-Grandmother

Great-Grandfather	Great-Grandfather

My Grandmother	My Grandfather

My Father

My Sibling	My Sibling

About Me

I was born in...

_____

_____

Which is near...

_____

_____

My family's address was

_____

_____

My birthday is

_____

My parents named me (Full Name)

_____

_____

About Me

They chose this name because...

_____

_____

My nickname was...

_____

_____

Other members of my family:

Brothers (including dates of birth)

_____

_____

_____

_____

_____

_____

About Me

Sisters (including dates of birth)

_____

_____

_____

_____

_____

_____

_____

Place Photo Here

About Me

Place Photo Here

Describe the photos in a few words...

_____

_____

_____

_____

About My Parents

My Dad (your great grandfather) was named...

_____

_____

He was born in...

_____

_____

My Mom (your great grandmother) was named...

_____

_____

She was born in...

_____

_____

About My Parents

How my parents met...

_____

_____

_____

They earned their living by...

_____

_____

_____

Things they enjoyed doing together...

_____

_____

_____

Their wedding anniversary was on...

_____

_____

About My Parents

Words to describe my mother...

_____

_____

_____

_____

_____

_____

_____

Words to describe my father...

_____

_____

_____

_____

_____

_____

_____

About My Parents

My mother's education...

_____

_____

_____

My father's education...

_____

_____

_____

My mother's interests...

_____

_____

My father's interests...

_____

_____

About My Parents

Things our family enjoyed doing together...

_____

_____

_____

_____

_____

_____

A family vacation we took together...

_____

_____

_____

_____

_____

_____

About My Parents

Traits I got from my mother...

_____

_____

_____

_____

_____

_____

Traits I got from my father...

_____

_____

_____

_____

_____

_____

A story I want to share about my family when I was growing up

_____

_____

_____

_____

_____

_____

_____

_____

_____

_____

_____

_____

_____

More about ME growing up

Things I was interested in...

_____

_____

_____

Hobbies...

_____

_____

My most favorite childhood memory...

_____

_____

_____

_____

_____

_____

_____

More about ME growing up

Favorite summer activities...

_____

_____

Favorite fall activities...

_____

_____

Favorite winter activities...

_____

_____

Favorite spring activities...

_____

_____

_____

More about ME growing up

My closest childhood friends…

_____

_____

_____

Household chores I'm responsible for…

_____

_____

Usual things I do on weekends…

_____

_____

_____

_____

_____

_____

More about ME growing up

My favorite childhood games...

_____

_____

_____

Your most precious toy...

_____

_____

What did you consider to be a real treat as a child?

_____

_____

_____

_____

_____

_____

More about ME growing up

I get scolded or grounded for...

_____

_____

_____

Things I'm good at...

_____

_____

Things I learned from my parents...

_____

_____

_____

_____

_____

_____

Do you remember having a happy childhood?

_____

_____

_____

_____

_____

_____

_____

_____

_____

_____

_____

_____

_____

_____

School Life

Where I attended school (from preschool to college)

_____

_____

_____

_____

Course I took in college

_____

_____

Things I liked about school

_____

_____

_____

_____

_____

_____

School Life

Things I disliked about school

_____

_____

_____

_____

My closest friends in my school days...

_____

_____

The people from my school days that I still keep in touch with

_____

_____

_____

_____

_____

_____

Your Grandfather and I

When and where we met and how it felt...

_____

_____

_____

_____

_____

_____

Was it love at first sight?

_____

_____

Things you loved doing together...

_____

_____

_____

Your Grandfather and I

Your grandfather's birthday...

_____

What you loved most about grandpa?

_____

_____

Do you remember how he proposed?

_____

_____

_____

Our wedding anniversary...

_____

Our best memories together...

_____

_____

_____

Your Grandfather and I

What we normally disagree on...

_____

_____

Funniest memories with grandpa...

_____

_____

_____

_____

His favorite food that I would cook...

_____

What was your wedding day like?

_____

_____

_____

Your Grandfather and I

Things we do to relax ourselves...

_____

_____

_____

_____

_____

What are the important elements of a happy relationship?

_____

_____

_____

_____

_____

_____

_____

Your Grandfather and I

Things your grandpa does that I appreciate

_____

_____

_____

_____

_____

Place Photo Here

Your Grandfather and I

Place Photo Here

Describe the photos in a few words...

_____

_____

_____

_____

About my child, your parent

Your parent's birthday

_____

Full name and why we chose this...

_____

_____

_____

_____

Traits he or she got from you...

_____

_____

_____

Traits he or she got from grandfather...

_____

_____

_____

About my child, your parent

Bad habits you consistently corrected...

_____

_____

_____

Traits I got from him or her...

_____

_____

_____

Place Photo Of You Two Together

Family Traditions & Holidays

Our family's favorite tradition and why...

_____

_____

_____

_____

How we celebrate birthdays...

_____

_____

_____

_____

How we celebrate anniversaries...

_____

_____

_____

_____

Family Traditions & Holidays

How we celebrate Easter...

_____

_____

_____

_____

How we celebrate 4th of July...

_____

_____

_____

_____

How we celebrate Thanksgiving...

_____

_____

_____

_____

Family Traditions & Holidays

How we celebrate Halloween...

_____

_____

_____

_____

How we celebrate Christmas...

_____

_____

_____

_____

How we celebrate New Year's...

_____

_____

_____

_____

Family Traditions & Holidays

Things we do during Spring...

_____

_____

_____

Things we do during Summer...

_____

_____

_____

Things we do during Fall/Autumn...

_____

_____

_____

Family Traditions & Holidays

Things we do during Winter...

_____

_____

_____

_____

Other family traditions passed from old generations...

_____

_____

_____

_____

The significance of these traditions to our family...

_____

_____

_____

_____

Family Traditions & Holidays

Photos from different holiday celebrations

Family Traditions & Holidays

Photos from different holiday celebrations

Family Traditions & Holidays

Photos from different holiday celebrations

Family Traditions & Holidays

Photos from different holiday celebrations

Family Recipes

Name: _____

Serves: _____ Prep Time: _____

Ingredients:

_____

_____

_____

_____

_____

Instructions:

_____

_____

_____

_____

_____

_____

Family Recipes

Name: _____

Serves: _____ Prep Time: _____

Ingredients:

_____

_____

_____

_____

_____

Instructions:

_____

_____

_____

_____

_____

_____

Family Recipes

Name: _____

Serves: _____ Prep Time: _____

Ingredients:

_____

_____

_____

_____

_____

Instructions:

_____

_____

_____

_____

_____

_____

Family Recipes

Name: _____

Serves: _____ Prep Time: _____

Ingredients:

_____

_____

_____

_____

_____

Instructions:

_____

_____

_____

_____

_____

_____

Family Recipes

Name: _____

Serves: _____ Prep Time: _____

Ingredients:

_____

_____

_____

_____

_____

_____

Instructions:

_____

_____

_____

_____

_____

_____

Family Recipes

Name: _____

Serves: _____ Prep Time: _____

Ingredients:

_____

_____

_____

_____

_____

Instructions:

_____

_____

_____

_____

_____

_____

Family Recipes

Name: _____

Serves: _____ Prep Time: _____

Ingredients:

_____

_____

_____

_____

_____

Instructions:

_____

_____

_____

_____

_____

_____

Family Recipes

Name: _____

Serves: _____ Prep Time: _____

Ingredients:

_____

_____

_____

_____

_____

Instructions:

_____

_____

_____

_____

_____

_____

Family Recipes

Name: _____

Serves: _____ Prep Time: _____

Ingredients:

_____

_____

_____

_____

_____

Instructions:

_____

_____

_____

_____

_____

_____

Family Recipes

Name: _____

Serves: _____ Prep Time: _____

Ingredients:

_____

_____

_____

_____

_____

Instructions:

_____

_____

_____

_____

_____

_____

Life & Living

What do you believe is the key to good health?

_____

_____

_____

_____

_____

_____

_____

What do you believe is the key to happiness?

_____

_____

_____

_____

_____

_____

Life & Living

What do you believe is the key to success?

_____

_____

_____

_____

_____

_____

What do you believe is the key to work-life balance?

_____

_____

_____

_____

_____

_____

Life & Living

What is your motto in life?

_____

_____

_____

_____

_____

_____

How do you live by this motto?

_____

_____

_____

_____

_____

_____

Life & Living

What are the things that make you happy?

_____

_____

_____

_____

_____

_____

Words of wisdom you'd like to impart...

_____

_____

_____

_____

_____

_____

Bucket List

List all of the things you'd like to do

_____

_____

_____

_____

_____

_____

_____

_____

_____

_____

_____

_____

_____

_____

Bucket List

List all of the things you'd like to do

_____

_____

_____

_____

_____

_____

_____

_____

_____

_____

_____

_____

_____

Bucket List

List all of the things / activities you'd like to do with me

_____

_____

_____

_____

_____

_____

_____

_____

_____

_____

_____

_____

_____

_____

Bucket List

List all of the things /activities you'd like to do with me

_____

_____

_____

_____

_____

_____

_____

_____

_____

_____

_____

_____

_____

About You and I

My first thought or thoughts when I learned I was going to be a grandmother

_____

_____

_____

_____

_____

_____

What did you do when it was announced to you?

_____

_____

_____

_____

_____

_____

_____

About You and I

Where I was when you were born...

_____

_____

_____

_____

_____

_____

The first thing I did with you...

_____

_____

_____

_____

_____

_____

About You and I

Our first photo together

What happened in this photo...

_____

_____

_____

_____

_____

About You and I

My earliest memory with you...

_____

_____

_____

_____

_____

_____

My favorite memory of you and I is...

_____

_____

_____

_____

_____

_____

About You and I

You and I when you were 1 month old

What happened in this photo...

_____

_____

_____

_____

_____

About You and I

You and I when you were 6 months old

The growth progresses you remember…

_____

_____

_____

_____

_____

About You and I

You and I when you turned 1

Remarkable things you remember...

_____

_____

_____

_____

_____

About You and I

You and I when you turned 7

Remarkable things you remember...

_____

_____

_____

_____

_____

About You and I

You and I when you turned 13

Remarkable things you remember...

_____

_____

_____

_____

_____

About You and I

You and I when you turned 16

Remarkable things you remember...

_____

_____

_____

_____

_____

About You and I

You and I when you turned 21

Remarkable things you remember...

_____

_____

_____

_____

_____

About You and I

More photos of you and I

Remarkable things you remember...

_____

_____

_____

_____

_____

About You and I

More photos of you and I

Remarkable things you remember...

_____

_____

_____

_____

_____

About You and I

More photos of you and I

Remarkable things you remember...

_____

_____

_____

_____

_____

About You and I

More photos of you and I

Remarkable things you remember...

_____

_____

_____

_____

_____

About You and I

Something that I've always wanted us to do together...

_____

_____

_____

_____

_____

Things I talked about with my children when they were your age...

_____

_____

_____

_____

_____

About You and I

Photo doing our favorite activities together

Remarkable things you remember...

_____

_____

_____

_____

_____

About You and I

Photo doing our favorite activities together

Remarkable things you remember...

_____

_____

_____

_____

_____

About You and I

Thanksgiving Photo

Remarkable things you remember...

_____

_____

_____

_____

_____

About You and I

Halloween Photo

Remarkable things you remember...

_____

_____

_____

_____

_____

About You and I

Christmas Photo

Remarkable things you remember...

_____

_____

_____

_____

_____

About You and I

New Year's Photo

Remarkable things you remember...

_____

_____

_____

_____

_____

About You and I

Things I wish I'd talked to them about...

_____

_____

_____

_____

_____

_____

_____

_____

_____

_____

_____

_____

About You and I

Things I enjoy talking to you about...

_____

_____

_____

_____

_____

_____

_____

_____

_____

_____

_____

_____

About You and I

Things I wish I knew about you...

_____

_____

_____

_____

_____

_____

_____

_____

_____

_____

_____

_____

About You and I

My greatest wishes for you as you grow...

_____

_____

_____

_____

_____

_____

_____

_____

_____

_____

_____

_____

My Letters To You

Date: _____

Special Event / Milestone: _____

_____

_____

_____

_____

_____

_____

_____

_____

_____

_____

_____

_____

My Letters To You

Date: _____

Special Event / Milestone: _____

_____

_____

_____

_____

_____

_____

_____

_____

_____

_____

_____

_____

My Letters To You

Date: _____

Special Event / Milestone: _____

_____

_____

_____

_____

_____

_____

_____

_____

_____

_____

_____

_____

My Letters To You

Date: _____

Special Event / Milestone: _____

_____

_____

_____

_____

_____

_____

_____

_____

_____

_____

_____

My Letters To You

Date: _____

Special Event / Milestone: _____

_____

_____

_____

_____

_____

_____

_____

_____

_____

_____

_____

_____

_____

My Letters To You

Date: _____

Special Event / Milestone: _____

_____

_____

_____

_____

_____

_____

_____

_____

_____

_____

_____

My Letters To You

Date: _____

Special Event / Milestone: _____

_____

_____

_____

_____

_____

_____

_____

_____

_____

_____

_____

My Letters To You

Date: _____

Special Event / Milestone: _____

_____

_____

_____

_____

_____

_____

_____

_____

_____

_____

_____

My Letters To You

Date: _____

Special Event / Milestone: _____

_____

_____

_____

_____

_____

_____

_____

_____

_____

_____

_____

My Letters To You

Date: _____

Special Event / Milestone: _____

_____

_____

_____

_____

_____

_____

_____

_____

_____

_____

_____